AF428269

So here's to the Event managers, brave and bold,
Who stay cool when things unfold.
No matter what, we stand so strong,
'Cause The Show Must Go On...
Even If Everything Else Goes Wrong!

THE SHOW MUST GO ON!

(Even If Everything Else Goes Wrong)

The Life of an Event Manager

Mohamad Gous

INDIA · SINGAPORE · MALAYSIA

ISBN
Hardcase 979-8-89906-629-0
Paperback 979-8-89744-975-0

Contents

Meet
the mind
behind the
words

Meet the Mind Behind the Words

Born and raised in the serene and picturesque state of Goa, surrounded by pristine beaches and lush nature, Mohamad Gous always dreamed of soaring through the skies as a pilot. However, fate had other plans, leading him down a different path, one that would be filled with creativity, energy, and unforgettable moments.

As the founder of **M&M Events, Goa** and the Director of **Amsa Group**, the event management and production house in Goa, Mohamad Gous has spent years shaping and orchestrating some of the most iconic events in India, from the grand stages of the **International Film Festival of India (IFFI)** to the thrilling atmosphere of **National Games**, from electrifying **EDM music festivals** to the ever-popular **big fat weddings**.

Through years of experience and an unwavering commitment to excellence, Mohamad Gous has made a name for himself in the world of event management, turning every event into a spectacular, once-in-a-lifetime experience. Now, he is embarking on a new adventure as an author writing his very first book.

If this book made you laugh, cry, or scream into a pillow (hopefully from laughter), tell Mohamad Gous! Slide into his DMs on Instagram **@Mohamad_07_97**. And if you found this book relatable… well, welcome to the chaos club!

Read This Before the Chaos Begins!
(Preface)

If you've ever organised an event, you know one thing for sure: something will go wrong. A missing vendor, a technical glitch, last-minute changes… anything can go wrong. But in the event management world, we follow one rule: The Show Must Go On! Even if everything else goes wrong.

In India, we're commonly referred to as **"tentwala"**, **"decorator"** and other terms which do not exactly justify the effort we put in. Event management is all about hard work and requires lots of skill, patience, and sleepless nights to make any event a successful one. Many don't see it as a serious profession. And the worst part? The majority of event managers never even get to share their struggles with the world.

That's why I wrote this book to show the behind-the-scenes chaos, struggle, hard work, creativity, craziness, and the real side of this profession. If you're an event manager, you'll relate to every page. If you're considering becoming one, you will know exactly what you're signing up for. If you simply love behind-the-scenes stories, you're in for a treat! And if you're about to hire an event manager for your next big event, you must read this book first! It might just change the way you see them.

So sit back, enjoy the chaos, and remember—no matter what happens, The Show Must Go On! Even if everything else goes wrong.

– Mohamad Gous

Acknowlededgment

This book came to life **in association with:**

AMSA GROUP

(Event Management and Production House)

A huge thank you to them for making this possible.

To coffee, for keeping me awake. To my friends and family, for pretending to listen while I ranted about event disasters. And to every event that turned into a glorious mess, Thank you for the inspiration.

Where no problem is too
big and no detail
is too small

– Event Manager

The Spark
My journey into Events

Event management is a mixture of chaos and creativity, a field that attracts those with a passion for organisation, problem-solving, and a love for designing. For many, the journey into event management starts with a moment of inspiration, an eye-opening experience, a chance encounter, or simply the realisation that creating memorable moments is something that they want to pursue as a career.

For me, it all started in the most unexpected way by being a part of an event management company, *"**Amsa Group**", the event management and production house* in Goa and creating thermocol artwork for an event back in 2013. I had no idea at the time that this would be the moment that would ignite a passion for the world of events. The detailed designs and the hours spent with great care and attention to detail crafting each piece of décor were just the beginning, but what truly captivated me was watching the entire event come together.

As the lights dimmed, the music swelled, and guests began to filter in, I saw something magical unfold. People were laughing, networking, dancing, and simply enjoying themselves, surrounded by an atmosphere created from scratch by a dedicated team. It wasn't just the physical elements - the décor, the ambience, the food - it was the entire experience. At that moment, I realised that this was what I wanted to do for the rest of my life.

What I didn't realise, however, was how much work was hidden behind the scenes. The countless emails, the tight deadlines, the endless coordination, and the pressure to deliver something exceptional every time—none of that was visible from the outside. This profession would require more than just creativity; it would demand resilience, flexibility, and an unyielding commitment to making sure every detail, no matter how small, was executed flawlessly.

But even with the sleepless nights and the ever-growing to-do lists, I knew one thing for sure: event planning was where I wanted to focus my energy. From that moment on, I was hooked.

Red Roses Nightmare!

I've planned and executed a lot of weddings, but this one? This one was something else.

So with a month to go until the big day, and countless meetings and presentations behind, the client approved the décor and everything else. My team and I got to work ensuring all the details and everything were locked and loaded. Everything was planned perfectly with the client's vision.

But as always, there were last-minute surprises.

One day before the wedding, when we were expected at the venue to begin the setup, the client simply dropped a surprise. The flowers for the wedding "should be only red roses." I froze. A single red rose was not in our plans. Why was he requesting this now, after weeks of discussions? "I saw a mandap on Instagram; it looked incredible. I want the same!" he said. I tried to explain to him over and over that we didn't plan for this. We had specifically ordered different flowers, and in Goa, fresh flowers come from neighbouring states, and getting this many red roses overnight was impossible. But the client didn't care. He wanted it. No matter what.

So, my team went on this crazy adventure. We searched every florist, roadside vendor, and market in Goa. We called vendors from other states. We managed to get the roses somehow, but after hours of fighting and an all-night effort.

Just when I thought it couldn't get any worse than this, disaster struck again. We were supposed to begin the setup at 5 am. That was the agreement. That was the schedule. Instead, we got let in at 1:30 pm, almost 8 HOURS LATE. The whole plan collapsed. Guests were scheduled to check in at 3 pm, and we had only one and a half hours to set up a lobby décor that would normally require at least 5-6 hours. I was forced to call in extra workers, accelerate everything and pray for a miracle.

And the venue itself? A complete nightmare. It was too small, with no designated storage area, and no service lift to get the materials to the terrace on the 7th floor where the mandap was to be built. My team carried every single item on their shoulders up the stairs to the 7th floor. Pure energy and stress is all I and my team were running on. But the worst was still to come, sir. After fighting through the crisis of the red rose and the disaster of the venue, I finally had my first meal in two days.

As I bit into the biryani, the music stopped. Then, the lights and complete silence. The couple was about to begin their entry when the entire venue went dark and silent. There was silence for 2–3 minutes. People were looking around, puzzled. The wedding was about to be ruined. I ran as if I was being chased by monsters. I got to know that the generator went off due to a technical glitch. I kept requesting the hotel to give us temporary electricity supply for just

10–15 minutes. They agreed after a lot of convincing. In the meantime, I rushed to the anchor and told him, "Make it part of the show. Make this a special moment." He took to the mic without hesitation and said, "Ladies and gentlemen, this blackout was anticipated! It is the most amazing moment for the bride and groom, and we wanted everyone to focus their attention on them. Now let's shine this evening up for our stunning couple!" The crowd cheered. And just like that, what should have been the worst moment of the night became one of the most unforgettable.

The couple? They still think it was all a pre-planned surprise. Finally, the wedding was over, the mandap was perfect, and for a moment, I thought I was finally free to take a breath.

Then came the worst disaster!

We had informed the client numerous times that we needed music licences (PPL, Novex, RMPL, IPRS). The cut-off time for sound was 10 pm sharp. But, the client refused to get the permissions. Finally, at 9 pm, just an hour before the deadline, guests arrived prepared to party. And then, the police arrived as if they were invited to the after-party. I got to know that the locals had made a noise pollution complaint, and the PPL licensing authority turned up with the police as they had got a hint that these wedding guests had not taken the licenses. For this also, the client blamed me. "You have no idea how to deal with this!" he said, as if it wasn't his fault for not having taken the permissions. Before I could even react, the bride's uncle came up to me, irritated. "HOW COULD YOU NOT GET THE MUSIC LICENCE? DO YOU KNOW HOW EMBARRASSING THIS IS?" he yelled, showing a finger at me.

I took a deep breath and explained that we had insisted many times that the licenses are a must, but the client refused, thinking we wanted to earn extras from it. The uncle looked at the client. "Is this true?" he asked his brother. The now-accused client stammered, "Uh… yeah… but… I thought blah…blah…." The uncle cut him off. "You THOUGHT?! All this could have been avoided if you had only listened to the event manager and taken the permissions!"

For the first time on that night, I felt a little justice.

But I had to intervene and negotiate, pay the fines, and convince the police to allow the party to continue at a lower volume. It wasn't great, but at least the night didn't end with a disaster. The wedding was finally over and we did it!

When it was time to pay, the client deducted a huge amount, citing the following because it was my fault: The delay of lobby décor (even though we got the venue late), the police raid (even though he ignored our warnings), and the missing décor (even though it wouldn't even have fit in the venue as we had informed him earlier). After all the stress, sleepless nights, and last-minute chaos, this was the final insult. But then came a message from the bride and groom. "You fulfilled our dream wedding. We will never forget this evening." And, in that instant, I recalled why I do what I do. Because, after all, the show must go on! Even if everything else goes wrong!

The masters of
making the impossible
possible!
– Event Manager

The Warm-Up Act Before the Main Event Steals the Show

Who is the one behind the scenes, making dreams come true with a flawless touch?

Who is the one who plans every detail… so you don't have to?

Who is the one who handles all the pressure... so you only feel joy?

Who is the one ready for every last-minute change done by you, every impossible request prompted by you…?

Who is the one who sacrifices sleep, misses their meals, forgets their own celebrations… just to make yours unforgettable?

When things go wrong, they rise.

When moments turn critical, they deliver your event.

When the world watches, they shine, not for their own glory, but for you.

The heartbeat of your big day. The mind behind the magic. The master of perfection…

They don't just create events; they craft emotions, build memories, and turn time into treasure.

They are the ones who never ask for the spotlight, this time...

This time, it's their turn to stand at the centre of the stage.

Yes! It's "your Event Manager."

Because every masterpiece has its maker.

Let's begin the story of the real heroes...

Lights. Action. Memories.

Let the show unfold!

Who needs coffee when you have an **event manager's adrenaline?**

– *Event Manager*

"Oh Wow, Planning Parties Must Be So Fun!"

Oh, honey. If only you knew.

Fun? Sure! But it's the kind of fun that brings stress, sweat, and a personal relationship with coffee and laptop at 3 am. Event management looks glamorous; there's the champagne, the flowers, the fog, the twinkling lights, laughter in the air. But guess what? Behind every glamorous party, there's a human disaster avoider fuelled by caffeine and panic: The Event Manager.

All event managers are like magicians, but instead of pulling rabbits and pigeons out of hats, we pull solutions, creativity, and decisions out of thin air while trying not to cry. We are the movers and shakers that no one acknowledges. This diary of an event manager's life will open up the dark truth behind this profession that very few know. A profession forged with intense focus, endless passion, and rock-solid strength.

As far as the outside world is concerned, event management is a world of perpetual luxury, fun, parties, laughter, and limelight. But the reality is quite different, my dear.

Picture this in your cryptic mind: bright chandeliers shimmering, lovely floral arrangements, jubilant crowds celebrating, music spilling like honey from its bottles, a buffet carefully arranged. But if you look behind the curtain of wonder, all you see is a hurricane of minute details, constant worry and anxiety anticipation. Just imagine yourself in the centre of all of this, not an invited guest, but the person who is planning and managing the event and holding all the delicate threads, ensuring not a single thread unravels.

It's a profession of unseen hands and sleepless nights, a tireless dance of creativity, artistry, and tiptoe determination. Every perfect event conceals a mountain of last-minute changes, disasters avoided and dreams shaped with detailed attention. This is the hidden pulse of event management, *the world where victory and defeat are defined in seconds, where precision and perfection are not just a thrill, but the essential requirement.*

Event managers are the unsung heroes of life's biggest moments, whether it's a wedding, birthday, reception or a social event, juggling love as they plan the symphony of dreams and details that becomes a picture-perfect memory for you. Outsiders catch a glimpse of the lights and laughter, but every event manager with experience understands that each seamless work hides a war zone of unexpected circumstances and real-time decisions.

This is not a profession for the faint-hearted. It takes more than creativity—it takes determination, superior organisational skills, and the ability to deliver under the pressure of time and with quality.

It's a profession of careful planning, real-time problem solving, dealing with unpredictable clients, and above all, keeping your cool when the world appears to be falling apart. Consider the madness of a corporate gala when a crucial shipment related to the décor setup vanishes only hours before the event, or a wedding in which the sound system fails seconds before the couple's grand entry.

Here is where the event manager enters, like a Ninja tan tan tada! Fixing everything, making it seem easy. Maintaining that illusion of perfection.

So it's not merely about addressing problems; it really is about doing so with such elegance that no one notices a thing. It's a daily war between chaos and control, but the only rule is, the guests must not see the battle.

The show must go on, even if we're quietly thinking of switching career paths to something more peaceful, **like wrestling sharks.**

If there's one thing to keep in mind about event management, it's that it's as thrilling as it is tiring. Event managers are not chasing their fame or recognition; they are chasing perfection. Not for their own sake, but to ensure someone else's big day is everything they dreamed it would be.

So next time you're at a glorious event, raise your glass not just to the celebration, but to the exhausted, over-caffeinated miracle worker who made it happen: The Event Manager.

Where calmness is
contagious
but stress is
infectious!
– Event Manager

Blueprint – The Foundation of it All

From Idea to Reality – The Puzzle of Event Planning

All events begin with an idea. Clients sketch a vision in broad strokes. To anyone outside the process, planning can appear to be a neat project of checklists and timelines. But in practice, it's more like a massive, constantly shifting puzzle, which keeps on changing so damn quickly until the celebration is over, ah!

What does an event manager do? Other than coming up with a beautiful idea, they have to develop that idea into practicality, in-depth with details. Imagine if there was a client saying, "We want something grand," but did not explain what "grand" means for them. It is up to the event manager to ask the right questions, consider the possibilities, and make that vision a real thing for all of those attending the event, a skill that takes both intuition and experience.

Midnight hits and still the work of the events manager isn't done. In the dim light of a laptop screen, you read through checklists, floor plans, and endless spreadsheets. A bride's request for "lights cascading like stars" solidifies into a detailed plan that covers wiring, placement, and safety checks.

Event planning is not only about making it look good; it's all about perfect timing. Think about putting on a production, making sure that the meals, music, and décor all blend seamlessly. It's a hustle of decision-making where one error can spoil months of effort. You prepare not only for the best case but for the worst case as well. A plan is only as good as its backup (or two).

Budgets – The Battle Between Dreams and Reality

Budgets are typically the most common obstructive and challenging element. Picture this: A couple imagines a royal wedding, with crystal chandeliers and elaborate fresh floral arches, but their budget leaves little room for even simple décor with artificial florals. This is where creativity steps in… Yeah!

With drapes, clever lighting, and painted pillars, I turned an ordinary venue into a palace-like venue, all on a tight budget. Guests were amazed! Proving that being creative and full of imagination can turn financial limits into stunning success.

Many clients frequently request ceiling flowers with chandeliers but want to pay as little as possible. It's a dance of balancing creativity and practicality with every conversation. Budget management isn't solely about slashing expenses but rather making every penny spent worth the investment while also keeping our clients happy.

Managing Teams & Handling Logistics

Leadership involves managing an event while the chaos lies in wait to take over. You have a team mix of talents that turn to you for guidance & approval.

Suppose you are coordinating an outdoor concert, especially in Goa, and dark rain clouds form. There's no time to panic. You send the team, you move equipment under cover, you map out paths, you adjust the schedule on the spot. That's the leadership take in event management, where you don't wait until things go wrong.

Budgeting? This is like juggling fire while walking a financial tightrope. You negotiate with vendors the way a diplomat negotiates getting the best possible deal while maintaining relationships. Leadership is about making rapid decisions and taking ownership of each one.

But beyond leadership, logistics is where the rubber meets the road, I mean where things get real.

Just imagine: It's a sunny afternoon, and a gorgeous outdoor wedding awaits in just a few hours. The guests are on their way, but the trucks with the stage décor are stuck in traffic. The bride's mother is anxiously looking at her watch.

The event manager doesn't panic, though anxiety starts pumping. There's a backup team clearing alternate routes for the trucks, extra flowers from local vendors are arranged and the layout of the ceremony is adjusted to prevent delays. And finally, with only moments to go, the stage is prepared, the takes bloom, and the music starts. Strangers have no clue about the chaos that nearly destroyed the day; what the strangers see is the beautiful stage setup and the air filled with love and music.

This event logistics is effortless for the guests, but for the event manager, it is a perfect storm of quick thinking, problem-solving, and teamwork behind the scenes.

Permits, transportation, safety checks, and all other steps need to be handled carefully as they are labelled as **fragile.** One mistake, a missing tablecloth, or a late vendor, can set off a mountain of problems. There are no do-overs in this business, sir; it's a one-chance, and you have to make it happen by hook or by crook. Every detail must be practised, every scenario planned because once the event begins, there's no going back.

Coordination: The Art of Holding It All Together

Think of it like being the only person in a room who actually knows what's going on at an event. Now, picture yourself; you have 20 different individuals simultaneously asking you 50 different questions. That's event coordination.

"You're like the Wi-Fi connection that holds everything together, and if you go down, so does the whole event."

Imagine a conductor leading an orchestra, and only instead of waving a baton, you're bringing together schedules, vendors and last-minute surprises. Your phone is blowing up all the time: vendors calling with delivery confirmations, caterers looking for a headcount, photographers asking for the face lights, anchors and performers needing stage cues and yes, the labourers asking for tea, food, water and whatnot!

You're their hands, their eyes, their ears, every moving piece, all rely on what you tell them. You hurry through the venues, nudging people softly through headsets. It all has to fall into place perfectly, not a second can be wasted.

And when the doors swing open, and guests enter into a universe that feels effortless, you finally exhale for a second. Ahhh!

The masters of multitasking,
juggling, & fire breathing!

– Event manager

Family Drama and the Madness of Indian Weddings

No event is as complicated, emotional and gloriously chaotic as an Indian wedding. It is like being in a tornado of love, tradition, and so many opinions, all kicking up around you.

An event manager steps into a household where each relative, from dada-dadi (paternal grandparents) and nana-nani (maternal grandparents), to chacha-chachi (paternal uncle-aunt) and mama-mami (maternal uncle-aunt) — has a voice that needs to be heard. The bride and groom might imagine themselves having a sleek, modern affair, while their parents, deeply rooted in traditions, dream of elaborate rituals and floral displays.

And what about phupha (paternal uncle) and bua (paternal aunt)—the masters of expressing displeasure over minute details? Phupha may want to set up the stage décor to his 100 percent specifications, and bua needs her favourites sitting in the centre near the dessert table. Meanwhile, mama recalls a grand wedding he attended in a foreign country and pushes for it to include exotic elements, while chachi fights for simplicity. Nana-nani and dada-dadi evoke nostalgia, recalling customs that "must not be forgotten."

As the noise gets louder, it's as if everyone wants to take the wedding over as if it's theirs. Ahh! The bride's brother will demand a grand baraat entrance with an exotic car, while the groom's cousins will ask for the best choreographer's number. Each is passionate and strong, and emotions fly high. Phewww!!!

In the middle of this roller-coaster, the event manager is a patient mediator, the measured maestro of family harmony. Every voice must be included, every feeling respected, and every wish delicately crafted into the fabric of the event."

Imagine the event manager getting banged in a storm of opinions, bua arguing that marigold garlands are non-negotiable and the bride wants white orchids. Phupha argues energetically about the seating arrangement; he wants his friends in the front row. In response, the event manager listens, nods, calms tempers, and provides compromises.

"We can frame the entrance with marigolds but include orchids as well. Yeah, I am smart, isn't it, blending traditional with modern elegance," they say, creating a peaceful cup of coffee in the middle of a war zone.

It's a performance of diplomacy, patience, and steadfast dedication to unity. The trick is to combine this potentially messy mix of wants into a smooth celebration so that phupha and bua are calm. Ha ha ha

Seating arrangements are emotional landmines as ancient family grudges and disputes over who gets to sit closest to the mandap surface. The napkin's colour sparks heated debate, the elders pick red for tradition, and the bride envisions dusky pastels to blend with her designer lehenga.

But the event manager stays cool throughout, making sure no one is left unheard. It takes hours to perfect every detail, even coordinating the flower colour with the bride's lehenga. Because in an Indian wedding, it's all about the details.

What do event managers and magicians
have in common? Making things happen
out of thin air!

– Event manager

How to Bend Without Breaking - Mastering Flexibility

Chaos is always lurking, just waiting to strike on the day of an event. No plan stands up to reality; a late vendor, an unexpected rainstorm, or an electrical failure can threaten to spoil months of planning. (I am crying here)

"As a beach lover, imagine an ideal wedding on a peaceful beach. Before the bride embarks on her walk down the aisle, dark clouds loom again, especially in Goa. Patrons whisper tensely as the first drops hit. Others might gasp in horror, but the event manager gets into the action like a Ninja tan tan tada! Tents are quickly constructed, chairs are shuffled, and backup lights are turned on. Very quickly, order is restored, and the wedding unfolds with streamlined elegance, with guests unaware of the near disaster."

Adaptability isn't only about responding to external forces; it's about being grounded in the eye of the storm when plans go wrong.

Think of a high-profile gala dinner. A keynote speaker's flight is delayed for hours. (you know which airline it is) The crowd gets restless, and the event threatens to lose its momentum. At that point, it's all hands on deck for the event manager, the crisis Ninja, rearranging speeches, adjusting entertainment, and even arranging for surprise guests to come around to keep your guests occupied. Each swift decision, each self-assured command, transforms disaster into a smooth performance. All this can only be done by an event manager. (These stunts are performed by trained event managers; please do not try this at home or anywhere)

It is the art of bending without breaking that truly marks this challenging profession. As an event manager, one must be prepared to expect things to go wrong and be cool enough to accommodate last-minute changes.

A groom might suddenly decide he wants a dramatic entrance on horseback. One even insisted that last-minute changes to audio-visuals be made. A vendor might not deliver an essential décor element (specially marigold garlands demanded by bua). But with quick thinking, steady hands and a relentless chase for answers, the event manager stitches each twist into the narrative unfolding before him.

Because in the events world, perfection isn't about avoiding chaos, but it's about solving them, before anyone else even notices.

Who needs superheroes
when you have
event managers?

– Event manager

Unseen Struggles Behind the Curtain

When others celebrate their day by enjoying dancing and drinking, the event manager sacrifices. Personal milestones pass by unnoticed, as you know the weekends and holidays blend into forever workdays. Birthdays are missed, and anniversaries are celebrated via fleeting text messages.

Imagine managing a multi-day destination wedding and watching your child blow out birthday candles via a video call. Welcome to the world of an event manager crafting happiness for others while sacrificing your own.

Hunger, Exhaustion and the Unbearable Pursuit of Perfection

Meals become a luxury. Imagine leaning against a bustling stage, orchestrating the many, many tiny details of a large event, all the while starving because you have no time to eat.

Imagine the event manager looking at the lavish buffet that has been prepared for the guests, stomach growling but unable to take a single bite because the show must go on. In the chaos of crafting perfection, a lukewarm cup of coffee serves as breakfast, lunch, and dinner. Sometimes, a soggy sandwich eaten between urgent phone calls is the only fuel source for us.

Yet hunger and exhaustion go ignored, overlooked by an unwavering commitment to get every detail crafted perfectly. As clients and their families celebrate on the dance floor, the event manager is often running on fumes, hyper-alert, and solving problems before they become disasters.

Because in this profession, there's no pause button, only the promise of a perfect event, at any expense.

The guardians of great experiences!

– Event manager

Clashes with Vendors and Gatekeepers

Vendors can be great partners, but they can also create headaches. Imagine an exciting, peaceful garden wedding. But the flowers, a centrepiece of the couple's vision, are nowhere to be found. Time is short, and guests are starting to arrive. A quick phone call reveals the florist misheard the time and is stuck in traffic, miles away.

The event manager springs into action, nervous but calm, dispatching another team to help, ordering last-minute flowers from neighbourhood vendors, and instructing the late florist on a quicker route to get set up before guests arrive. Finally, with seconds to spare, the arches blossom with fresh flowers, and no one in the assembled audience has an idea of the chaos that had threatened to spoil the day.

Vendors are easy to manage in theory, but they need some diplomacy to keep their relations non-psychotic, some firmness to enforce the contracts they sign, and stubborn beings to solve the problems that arise in their execution. In this tightrope act of collaboration and conflict, each engagement determines the event's eventual success. A reliable florist who suddenly sends the wrong arrangement or a caterer whose staff shows up late can spoil months of planning.

It's a bureaucratic war to get permits for music, sound and safety, at times. Imagine a wedding in the open air, where sound restrictions turn off the music at midnight. The guests, appearing fashionably late, are still deep into their dinner. Police patrol the surroundings, ready to enforce the rules. When it goes quiet, the event manager is to blame, but never mind that everyone knows the rules.

And yet, through all this chaos, who gets blamed if anything goes wrong? That's right, you event manager, you! The music stops. "Why didn't you fix it?" The police show up. "You should have handled it!" The bride's uncle stumbles on a carpet. "How do you let this happen?!"

And don't get me started on music licences: PPL, NOVEX, RMPL, IPRS. If clients hear anything about it, they suddenly become experts in loopholes. "Do we really need that?" they ask. BANG, the cops cut the speakers.

So we juggle, negotiate, and problem-solve, so the client can dance the night away... completely unaware of the storm we just settled.

Vendors, permits, and last-minute disasters; somehow, it's always the event manager stuck in the middle, performing miracles while the rest of the world enjoys the show.

Where **creativity** meets chaos!
– Event manager

Financial Struggles and the Sweet Satisfaction of Surviving

The glamour of events makes it seem that event management is a very profitable business. But the financial rewards the book describes are often overshadowed by financial risks behind the scenes.

Envision the heart-racing moment when a bride's family demands at the 11th-hour, bespoke flower arrangements flown in from overseas. But the event manager will bear the indirect costs by dipping into personal savings without hesitation. A winner in this space is not one who just cashes in; it's one who solves problems, takes risks, makes decisions on the spot, and guarantees perfection no matter the cost.

Margins are paper-thin, and surprises can be costly. Imagine this for one more time, please. The bride's family suddenly decides that the wedding mandap needs an upgrade with imported flowers and designer lighting. With no time for negotiation, the event manager, placing the utmost importance on making the client happy, pays out-of-pocket for the extras to make sure everything goes absolutely right. These are not unique personal sacrifices. In this world where profit isn't king, the integrity of the event is placed above all other concerns.

In addition to the financial strain, there's the emotional roller coaster. When things may not go as perfectly as planned, clients can make demands that really are impossible or blame where blame does not belong when minor hiccups occur. But all that fatigue, near-misses, and 11th-hour repair fixes culminate in one remarkable instant when a father of the bride, eyes brimming with thankfulness, grips the event manager's hand and says those seven words: "Thank you for making this day perfect."

In that moment, all of the sacrifices seem worth it. But let's make one thing clear: event managers have bills to pay as well! This isn't a Bollywood movie where we do it all for the love of art. Fire in our belly, for sure, but fire in our belly doesn't pay venue deposits or vendor fees. Event management doesn't have a price, but they do need to be compensated well for the magic they craft. Because at the end of the day, we don't just create dreams; we have a life to live too.

The architects
of amazing
experiences!

– Event manager

Grading Chaos – Turning Every Oops into a Lesson

When the applause fades, and the guests disperse, the work of the event manager is far from done. That's when the real growth takes place, not in the spotlight but in the quiet moments. Every event is a lesson, and the best event managers don't move on; they reflect, analyse, and improve.

You gather your team after an event, a touch of exhaustion and pride in the atmosphere. You review each detail together, like assembling a puzzle.

Did the event run on schedule, or were there any lags? Was the lighting just okay, or did it actually change the mood? Did the flow of cues go in a timely manner and was it entertaining?

Every little thing matters because, I mean, even small things can leave a big impact in this industry. You listen when people compliment you and when they complain about you. Recognising that feedback, even when it stings, is a gift that can be used to help you grow.

You don't react to criticism personally; you learn from it to make the next occasion even better. If it doesn't work out, it's not a failure; it's a lesson. If one thing worked out, it's not an excuse to relax and chill; it's the new standard to beat next time.

Every event teaches you something new with that effort and struggle. Over the period of time, you begin to develop sharper instincts, better planning skills and yes the ability to solve problems quickly. Success isn't just about one perfect event but it's about constantly learning and improving. In this profession, you don't just improve, but in fact, you become extraordinary with every challenge you overcome.

Where every event is a **new challenge** and a **new opportunity!**

-Event manager

The Secret Agents of Event Chaos

The last dance ends, the confetti falls, and silence returns. You stand in the shadows. You are the magician behind the curtain, the creator of memories that will last a lifetime. There is not a spotlight on you, and that's not why you do it. Your pride lies not in being recognised but in the happiness you are able to bring to the people, the memories you help plant as a permanent fixture in the hearts of people forever.

But this is not a role built on fleeting glamour. It requires long hours of preparation, sacrifices made behind a posed smile, and the ability to be cool when the intensity is at boiling point. You are the first one to show up and the last one to leave, walkie-talkie strapped to your side, your eyes roaming over every detail in every place. You don't merely coordinate events but in fact, you give them soul. Every table setting, every beam of light, and every note of music reflects back the labour, effort, and precision you put into every moment.

As the music fades, you watch families hug, colleagues celebrate, and dreams become true in front of you. And yet, few will ever know you by name. They'll remember the sparkle of the décor, but not the sleepless nights, the tight deadlines, or the behind-the-scenes sacrifices. They won't know about the family moments you missed or the fatigue you fought through because quitting was never an option for you as an event manager.

Guests leave with photographs and smiles; you leave with something a little different, though the quiet satisfaction of knowing that you turned what could have been an average day into something wonderful, which would have been impossible without your guiding hand.

Being an event manager of any event is a labour of love, an exercise in perfectionism wrapped in a storm of unpredictability. It's about finding joy in creating moments of connection for others, even if you're standing unseen behind the curtain. And while you are the hero of our story, unseen as always, you wear your title with pride. You are the unsung superhero behind every tear of joy, every resounding applause, and every joyous memory. You are the silent victory in your relentless efforts.

Do You Know? Titanic Would Have Been a Pool Party, if only Event Managers Were There!

Just imagine a world without event managers. A world where weddings become food fights, concerts go off without a band and corporate events forget to invite their CEO for the launch event of their new product. A world where important details are forgotten, schedules don't exist, and absolute chaos takes over. Sounds terrifying, right? Well, here's the good news: we have event managers! They ensure that everything runs like clockwork, even in the worst circumstances.

Now, About the Titanic…

Would the Titanic have sunk if they had event managers on board? Hmm, probably yes. But it would have been the most orderly and well-coordinated ship accident in history.

Backup plan? Oh, Absolutely! An event manager would have ensured there were Plan B, C and even D. Lifeboats? Extras would've been there, clearly labelled, assigned, and booked hours ahead, like VIP seating. Rather than a full panic, passengers would be handed a properly planned evacuation itinerary. There would have been a lifeboat check-in station, a fast-track queue for families, and a firm but friendly event assistant telling first-class passengers, "Sir, I don't care how rich you are, kindly board Lifeboat no. 6 according to the schedule."

Jack and Rose's Love Story? Wow, A Grand Love Affair! With an event manager on board, Jack would not have been left shivering in the sea as Rose comfortably stretched out on a large floating piece of wood. There would have been more life rafts, strategically placed, and an "Endless Romance" package to make sure their love story would go on and on… Jack and Rose wouldn't have needed to so dramatically cling to each other in ice water. Instead, they'd be safely seated on a well-prepared rescue raft, drinking hot chocolate passed out by the event team. While the lifeboats rowed away to safety, a strategically seated violinist (have I mentioned I am an event planner?) would softly play their love theme while Jack proposed exactly on the spot. "Rose, will you marry me?" he'd say, ring in hand, because what else would the event manager have brought along, an emergency proposal kit, in case the worst happened?

Once safely on land, the event crew would have organised their wedding, a lavish ocean-themed event with a cake shaped like an iceberg (too soon?) and proper music and dance without any breaks. VIP seating would be arranged so that the unsinkable Molly Brown could deliver a speech, and guests would receive elegant "I Survived the Titanic" party favours… It would be the wedding of the century because tragedy can be transformed into a spectacular event with the right planner in charge!

Iceberg? No problem! Okay, maybe avoiding the iceberg was out of their hands. But at least an event manager would have dealt like a pro. Rather than screams and chaos, there will be a cool, collected announcer: "Dear passengers, due to an exciting new 'Arctic Adventure' feature, we warmly encourage you to make your way to your assigned lifeboats in an orderly fashion." Life jackets would be handed out in matching colours to your outfit, and the band wouldn't play a sad song; instead, they'd perform I Will Survive to keep spirits high. event managers, The crisis ninjas save the day, be it a wedding, a business event, a music festival, or, for goodness' sake, maybe even a sinking ship. Without them, we'd be lost, probably at an event with no food, no directions, and a slideshow stuck on the first slide.

Who needs a superpower when you have
event **management skills?**

–Event manager

Brace Yourselves, Event Managers, Here's a Poem Just for you (Because Therapy is Damn Expensive)!

Behind the scenes, a mastermind, the Event Manager, one of a kind.

With plans and lists they take the stage, Coordinating details, turning the page.

From venues to vendors, to timelines so fine, they weave a web of perfection, a wondrous design.

Their attention to detail, a work of art. A symphony of logistics beating in their heart.

You have no tricks to play. You have no other story to tell.

The Event Manager, a conductor so grand, bringing people together with a skilful hand.

So this is for the event managers, the unsung heroes always true, who bring joy & magic, for both me and you.

May their events be flawless, their stress levels be low, and their passion for planning forever continue to glow.

– Event Manager

A Decree of Utmost Importance to Our Cherished Clients!

From: The land of sleepless nights,
caffeine-fuelled creativity;
and last-minute miracles—yes, you guessed it;
Your ever-dedicated Event Manager!

Date: Shubh Muhurat (Auspicious Time)

To: The One Who Wants,
a Grand Event Without Chaos,
(A.K.A. Our Beloved Client),

Subject: Your Event, Our Passion—A Slightly Dramatic but Very Honest Letter from Your Event Manager.

Oh, Glorious and Occasionally Mysterious Client,

First and foremost, congratulations on your upcoming event! We are as excited as you are, maybe even more (because our reputation is at stake). But before the confetti starts falling and the dance floor heats up, let's have a little heart-to-heart, shall we?

Lights. Camera. Action!

Let's get one thing straight: no event manager, big or small, ever wakes up and says, "You know what? Today, I'm going to ruin someone's big day." Nope! We are here to create magic, not chaos. But sometimes, the universe conspires against us.

A sudden downpour at an outdoor wedding? "Cue dramatic thunder sound!" A power failure in the middle of the grand sangeet? "Cue collective gasp from the audience!" A technical glitch during a high-profile corporate event? "Cue the event manager sprinting like Usain Bolt to fix it!" These are nightmares for any event planner, but we don't run away. We fight back like heroes in a climax scene, ensuring that The Show Must Go on! (Even if everything else goes wrong).

Do you know that sometimes, when a vendor backs out last minute, we put our own money in, just so your event doesn't suffer? Do you know that when you demand an elaborate setup overnight, we work round the clock, surviving on caffeine and hope? Do you know that when you suddenly add 100 extra guests, we don't faint (although we want to) but instead magically arrange everything as if we had Aladdin's magic lamp?

Your last-minute changes, unplanned demands, and sudden upgrades, though understandable, sometimes push us into chaos. But we do it anyway because your event is our event. Your happiness is our success. But please, dear client, don't make us go full-on "Khatron Ke Khiladi" mode every single time.

Now, let's talk about the forbidden word—BUDGET!

When a doctor asks about your medical history, you don't lie. When a lawyer asks for case details, you don't hide facts. Then why keep secrets from your event manager? We're not your in-laws; we won't judge you!

The biggest challenge we face is when a client wants a royal wedding but has a budget for a chai-samosa party. When we ask, "What is your budget?" it is not because we want to rob you. It is because we want to give you the best possible experience within your comfort zone. If we know your budget, we can suggest what suits you best without unnecessary expenses.

An event manager is not a magician who can pull a luxurious wedding out of thin air with a limited budget. Nor are we villains trying to make you overspend. We simply want to create the best event for you without unnecessary compromises.

Ah, payment! The most suspenseful part of our story. Now, let's be honest—when you book a hotel room, do you tell them, "I'll pay after I enjoy my stay"? When you book a banquet hall, do you say, "Let's see how the food tastes first"? No! You make the payment upfront because that's how businesses work.

Yet, somehow, when it comes to event managers, payments magically become optional, negotiable, or "We'll settle it after the event." No, my dear clients, this is not a Bollywood movie where we work for the love of the art alone. Payments need to be made on time, as per the agreed timeline, so that we can ensure everything is executed smoothly.

Delaying payments means delays in bookings, delays in arrangements, and last-minute chaos. And trust me, an event manager running behind vendors for payments is not a scene you want to witness—it's more tragic than any Bollywood breakup!

So, let's keep things professional, timely, and fair, and ensure that payments happen just as smoothly as your event.

An event manager is just as important as a doctor, an engineer, or a lawyer. We hold the responsibility of handling the most crucial days of your life. But unlike other professions, our industry is often taken for granted. People expect us to deliver miracles without acknowledging the hard work, expertise, and dedication that go into it.

So, dear boss, the next time you hire an event manager, please remember:

1. Trust us: We are here to make your event a grand success, not to ruin it.
2. Be transparent: Be honest about your budget and expectations so we can deliver what's best for you.
3. Plan ahead: Last-minute changes cause stress and problems that could be avoided with better communication.
4. Respect the process: Events are not magic; they require detailed and careful planning, coordination, and execution.
5. Recognise our efforts: Just like any other professional, we deserve appreciation for the time, energy, and creativity we invest.

The Show Must Go on! (Even if everything else goes wrong). But let's work together to ensure that it goes on smoothly, beautifully, and memorably. Because, at the end of the day, your joy is our ultimate standing ovation!

Thanking you for your patience (and for reading this far),

Yours sincerely,

____

The Master of Events, the Juggler of Last-Minute Changes, and Your Humble Event Manager, Your Ever-Dedicated Event Manager.

Lights off. Curtains down. But our dedication? That never ends.

That's a Wrap (No, Really, It's Over Now)

Event management isn't just a profession, but it's a roller-coaster of creativity, patience, strength, and love, culminating in an often never-ending chase for perfection. Imagine the event manager, the invisible mastermind, who creates miraculous moments out of chaos, their heartbeat

quickening as they transform disaster into wonder within a few seconds. From fixing clashing décor to calming family fights and from cooking fairy-tale dinners to making sure kids who come to the frosty night get the Santa gifts, this silent symphony plays in the background to turn dreams into reality. Event managers are the unsung heroes behind every blushing bride, every glamorous celebration, and every precisely timed firework. These behind-the-scenes ninjas work to make sure everything is perfect in the light.

This career isn't about applause or praise. It's about love for beauty, in the middle of chaos, and for the incomparable pleasure of making someone's dreams come true. It's about sleepless nights, unwavering dedication and the pleasure of knowing that when the curtain goes up, everything is as smooth as butter.

And next time you stand under a canopy of lights, lost in the magic of the moment, remember the hands and hearts that put it there. Event managers are the creators of joy, the builders of memories, and the heart of any celebration.

And really, as any event manager will tell you: "The show must go on! Even if everything else goes wrong."

Be Like an event manager!

And with that, the event is finished. The stage stands empty, the guests have dispersed, and what remains is a floor littered with confetti and one tired event manager, still smiling like a warrior "who survived" another war. But before we roll the credits, let's pause to spotlight the real takeaways here.

An event manager isn't just a person running around the venue with a clipboard, shouting into a walkie-talkie and wearing the look of someone who hasn't slept in days (which, to be honest, they haven't). So nope, my lovely readers, an event manager's life is full of roller-coasters!

You think your job is stressing you out? What about organising an event where the bride's lehenga is stuck in some traffic, the sound system has decided to go take a nap, and the cake is delivered looking like it has been through an earthquake? Event managers don't just fight stress; they dance with it! They know that even when things are bad, panic never does any good. (Though an occasional windy sigh is permissible.) Picture this: if we all adopted this mindset in our lives! Late for work? Spill coffee on your shirt? Just smile and say to the nation, "We'll fix it!"

Life is a DJ who will play funeral songs at a birthday party. But does the event manager scream and run? No! They take the mic, make a joke, and turn it into a memory. Their superpower is adaptability. If we learned to face the chaos of life like an event manager, we would invest less energy fussing and fuming, and more time enjoying.

Just like life, events give you surprises. A missing guest speaker, a venue with a sudden change in policy, or an uncle who has suddenly determined he'd like to give an impromptu, hour-long speech. But event managers? They're the human equivalent of Google Search, always ready with a backup plan. Likewise in life, we too must be ready for something without thinking much about it. Lost your job? Flight cancelled? Never mind, there is always another way!

Do you have any idea whether an event manager can afford to hold grudges? If we wrote down every guest who switched tables the day before, or every vendor who "forgot" to bring a little extra seating, we would need an entire library for our complaints! But nope, we smile, we forgive, we move on. Because at the end of the day, it is a profession about making people happy. Can you imagine if we all did this in real life, more love, less drama would have been there!

The only job of an event manager is to ensure that everyone is having fun. They'll run, sweat, negotiate and yes, even cry (in a corner, silently) so YOU can have the big day you dreamt about. What if that's how we all lived? What if it were less about scoring points and more about sharing joy? The world would be a much better place.

So, dear reader, the next time life throws a last-minute surprise, ask yourself: "What would an event manager do?"

They'd breathe deeply, put on their best smile, and make sure the show must go on, even if everything else goes wrong. And so should you!

Now, if you'll pardon me, I need a nap. The next event is in six hours.

The End or just the beginning of handling life like a pro event manager!

Applause, Confetti, and Probably a Cake!

Event Managers' Day, May 31st

It's the unsung heroes of creating memories…

The architects of celebration…

The dream-weavers, great experience-makers, and magic creators…

It's your event manager and the entire Event Industry who keep their lives on hold to bring your moments of joy to life.

Get ready because May 31st is Event Managers' Day, the new Favourite Day of the Year! This is not a date randomly dropped into the calendar. Nope. It's a day to shout out major appreciation for the people who make our festivities happen, and let's be honest, who doesn't love a good celebration? It's a day to honour the magic, the hard work, and the creative force of event managers, the minds behind every glamorous event we attend.

It's basically like one massive, global thank-you note to the pros that make even the simplest events extraordinary. Whether it's a wedding, a festival, a corporate event or even a birthday bash, these are the ones working tirelessly behind the scenes, making sure everything runs smoothly so we can just show up and enjoy the show. Can you believe it? Most of those so-called "perfect" moments we often take for granted would never have happened without them!

And here's where it gets even cooler: This day isn't just about honouring these rock stars for their hard work; it's also a full-on celebration of the art of celebration itself! It's about realising that building a party isn't just throwing up some décor and snacks, but moments that stay with you, memories that stay around long after the party has ended. It is meant to recognise the fact that the magic we feel at events is created by the crazy amounts of skill, thought, and hustle that are poured into them. Event managers don't make parties, but they make memories that we carry with us.

And if you consider other global celebrations like Father's Day, Mother's Day, or even Valentine's Day, they all have one thing in common: they're an opportunity to express love and gratitude to the amazing people who enrich our own lives. The same goes for Event Managers' Day. It's our turn to show gratitude to those unsung warriors who make sure everything is in place, from the aesthetics of the venue to the final dance. Without them, those unforgettable moments wouldn't be what they are.

Now, let's talk about the roots of this day. India, the land of a million festivals, vibrant weddings, and celebrations that go on for days, is where Event Managers' Day first came to life. In a country where every occasion is a grand event, it was only fitting to dedicate a day to the people who bring these celebrations to life. India has a long tradition of creating larger-than-life celebrations, and it was only natural that this special day would be born from its rich cultural history.

But here's the thing: India didn't keep this gem to itself. Nope! It decided to gift the world Event Managers' Day, and now, countries around the globe celebrate it on May 31ˢᵗ. It's like a beautiful, international tradition that reminds us all to appreciate the hard work, creativity, and love that go into making every event a once-in-a-lifetime experience. So next time you attend an event that blows your mind, remember: someone made that happen.

On **May 31ˢᵗ**, the stage is theirs.

It's Event Managers' Day, a day to honour their relentless efforts, their sleepless nights, and their unshakeable passion.

So, who will stand with us to give them the love, respect, and applause they deserve?

Who will recognise the souls who work so hard for your happiness yet never ask for the spotlight?

Join the celebration. Share the gratitude. Let's make the world remember… because behind every beautiful memory, there's an event manager making it happen.

Want to know more? Don't just sit there, hop over to www.eventmanagersday.com! It's like a virtual roller-coaster but with less screaming and more info.

A Note to the Legends Reading This

Dear Reader,

Thank you for joining me on this roller-coaster ride called ***The Show Must Go On! (Even If Everything Else Goes Wrong).***

This book is packed with all the chaos, heart, and caffeine-fuelled madness that make event management what it is. Sure, it looks all fancy and glamorous from the outside, but behind the scenes, it's a wild mix of last-minute changes, endless planning, and pure determination to turn ideas into jaw-dropping moments.

I've spilled my stories, lessons, and personal mishaps not just to show the reality of this crazy profession but also to remind you that no dream is too big (or too ridiculous) to chase. Life's best adventures usually start when you least expect them—just like my journey into events did!

Whether you're an aspiring event pro, looking for inspiration, or just wondering what really happens backstage, I hope this book gives you some laughs, insights, and a newfound respect for the magic-makers behind the scenes.

Remember, every event tells a story, and behind each one is a team making the impossible happen. Thanks for letting me share my story with you!

With gratitude and a to-do list that never ends.

– Mohamad Gous

www.ingramcontent.com/pod-product-compliance
Lightning Source LLC
Chambersburg PA
CBHW040853110726
48005CB00001B/46